Dear Mom,

In 2004, my mother became seriously ill. I realized then that I still had so many questions for her. About who she used to be, about her dreams, big and small. I also realized I hadn't told her often how important she was to me. That's when I created *My Mother's Book*, a book of questions I had about her life. It was my way of saying how much I loved her.

I'll never forget the day she gave the finished book back to me. I was hoping to get answers to my questions. I got back so much more. My mom loved filling out the book, sharing pictures I'd never seen and stories I'd never heard before. What once was an empty book had become the most precious gift I will ever receive in my life: the story of my mom and me.

After I shared the book with others, it soon became clear that I wasn't alone in my experience with my mother. Over the years, I've heard many stories about *My Mother's Book*, from mothers and children who have loved learning to connect, share, and remember. It's made the book even more special.

You're receiving *My Mother's Book* because you're special to the person who has given it to you. Normally, we don't return presents to the giver. This book is an exception. I like to call it a "Give and Get Back Book." It is my hope that you'll answer the questions, then return the book to the person who gave it to you.

My dream is that all mothers will complete this book and, in doing so, leave behind something valuable for their children. Something lasting, permanent. For always.

Lots of love,
Elma van Vliet

MY
MOTHER'S
BOOK

MY MOTHER'S BOOK

ELMA VAN VLIET

PENGUIN BOOKS

For all children who receive the completed book:

Enjoy reading your mother's stories.
I hope this becomes a true voyage of discovery.
About her, then and now, and about everything.

A NOTE FOR MOM

This is your book and your story. Feel free to make it completely your own!

You can decide how much and how often you write.

Rewrite questions if you'd like to answer them differently.

Add pictures you'd like to share.

Whatever feels right to you.

When you're done, give the book back to your daughter or son.

You've just shared a lifetime of you with someone who loves you.

CHILDHOOD

ABOUT BEING A CHILD 2

ABOUT YOUR (GRAND)PARENTS 12

ABOUT YOUR FAMILY 26

ABOUT GROWING UP AND

BECOMING AN ADULT 40

TELL ME SOMETHING ABOUT ME 56

GROWING UP

ABOUT LOVE 66

ABOUT BECOMING A MOTHER 78

TELL ME SOMETHING ABOUT ME 88

ALL YOUR FAVORITES

ABOUT SPARE TIME,

HOBBIES, AND TRAVELING 96

TELL ME SOMETHING ABOUT ME 110

WHO YOU ARE NOW

ABOUT MEMORIES 118

ABOUT THOUGHTS, WISHES, AND DREAMS 130

TELL ME SOMETHING ABOUT ME 146

CHILDHOOD

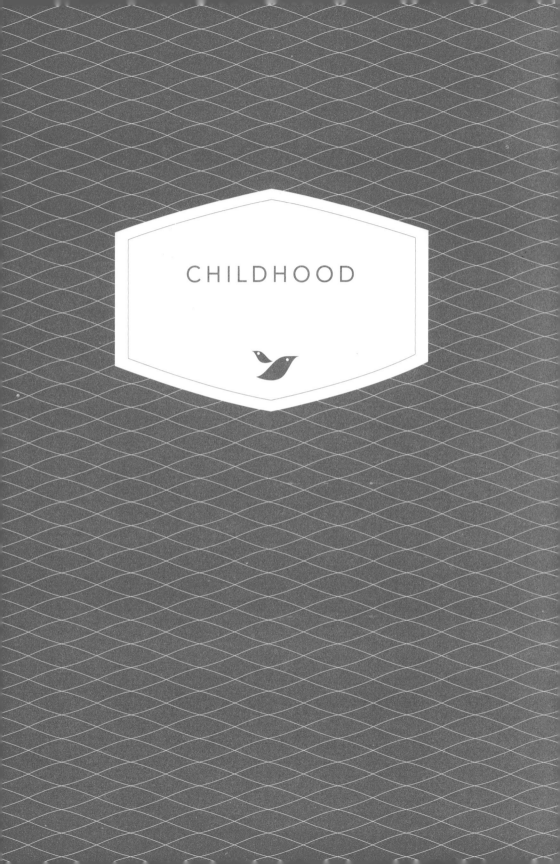

ABOUT BEING A CHILD

What day were you born? Were you born at home or in a hospital? _____

_____

_____

_____

_____

_____

What is your full name? _____

Do you know
why your
parents picked
your name?

_____

_____

_____

_____

_____

_____

_____

_____

What were your nicknames? _____

_____

_____

_____

What were you like as a child?

What games of make-believe did you play as a child?

Did you ever
pretend to be
a superhero?
Which one?

ABOUT BEING A CHILD

How do you remember your childhood?

Did you, for
example, have
a favorite toy
that you brought
everywhere?

What people or things were important to you?

What illnesses did you have as a child?

Did you ever
have to stay in
the hospital?

What were your favorite games?

Did you play inside the house, or did you like to go outside?

ABOUT BEING A CHILD

Who was your favorite playmate? _____

_____

_____

_____

_____

_____

_____

_____

_____

What was your favorite day of the week? _____

_____

_____

_____

_____

Why was
this day
so special
to you?

_____

_____

_____

_____

And your favorite day of the year?

Why was it
so special?

a page for
pictures . . .

a page for
pictures . . .

... and more stories
and memories

11

ABOUT YOUR (GRAND)PARENTS

What are your parents' names? _____

_____

_____

_____

Where and when were they born? _____

_____

_____

_____

Where and when were your grandparents born? _____

Grandmother and grandfather on your mother's side: _____

_____

_____

_____

_____

Grandmother and grandfather on your father's side: _____

_____

_____

_____

_____

Did you know your grandparents? Did you visit them often?

How was your extended family important to you while growing up?

ABOUT YOUR
(GRAND)PARENTS

What were different family members known for?

Was anyone
in your family
famous?

Who was the black sheep?

What did your parents do for a living?

And your grandparents?

ABOUT YOUR
(GRAND)PARENTS

What kind of parents were your parents?

Were they
modern
or more
old-fashioned?

How would you describe their relationship?

Was it a
traditional
one?

What role did religion play in your parents' lives?

ABOUT YOUR
(GRAND)PARENTS

How did your parents spend their free time? _____

_____

_____

_____

_____

_____

_____

_____

_____

_____

_____

_____

_____

Do you look more like your mother or your father? _____

What features and traits did you inherit from each? _____

How can
you tell?
_____

_____

_____

_____

What are the most important life lessons your parents taught you?

What activities did you enjoy doing with your mother? What did you talk about?

And with your father?

ABOUT YOUR
(GRAND)PARENTS

What kind of mother was your mother?

Can you share some cherished memories about your mother?

What kind of father was your father?

Can you share some cherished memories about your father?

a page for
pictures . . .

. . . and more stories
and memories

a page for
pictures . . .

... and more stories
and memories

25

ABOUT YOUR FAMILY

How many children did your parents have? _____

What are your brothers' and sisters' names? When were they born? _____

_____

_____

_____

_____

_____

_____

_____

Growing up, who did you spend the most time with? _____

How close
were you
to your
siblings?

_____

_____

_____

_____

_____

_____

Did you have any family pets? If so, what type? What were their names? _____

_____

_____

_____

What kind of family were you?

Did you
like spending
time at
home?

How did you help around the house?

ABOUT YOUR FAMILY

Were there activities you always did together? What were they? _____

_____

_____

_____

_____

_____

_____

_____

What TV shows or movies did you watch together? What books did you read together? _____

What
shows did
you enjoy
most?

What games did you like to play together? _____

_____

_____

_____

_____

What kind of house did you live in? What was the address?

Did you
ever move?

What did your room look like? Was it your own or did you share it?

What have you held on to from your childhood home?

ABOUT YOUR FAMILY

What kind of neighborhood did you grow up in? _____

_____

_____

_____

Did you
know your
neighbors? _____

_____

_____

_____

_____

How did you celebrate your birthday? _____

_____

_____

_____

_____

_____

_____

What was the best birthday present you ever received? _____

_____

_____

_____

What was your favorite food? And what did you hate?

What kind of food did your parents make? Do you cook like them now?

Are there
any dishes you
still make the
same way your
parents used to
make them?

ABOUT YOUR FAMILY

Did you ever go on family vacations or take any trips? Where did you go?

Which of these outings still brings a smile to your face?

What were your favorite stay-at-home moments?

How did you celebrate the holidays?

What other special days did your family observe?

ABOUT YOUR FAMILY

As a family, how did you communicate your feelings?

Did you
talk a lot
or very
little?

What hard times did you go through as a family?

Can you share some fond family memories?

a page for
pictures . . .

... and more stories
and memories

a page for
pictures . . .

. . . and more stories
and memories

ABOUT GROWING UP AND BECOMING AN ADULT

What elementary school did you go to? _____

_____

How did you get to school each day? _____

_____

Who was your favorite teacher? _____

_____

Why was
she or he
special to
you?

_____

_____

_____

Did you have a teacher you hated? How come? _____

_____

_____

_____

_____

_____

Were you a model student or did you dislike school?

What did you want to be when you were grown up?

Who were your best friends in elementary school?

Do you still keep in touch with them?

41

ABOUT GROWING UP AND BECOMING AN ADULT

What was your favorite thing to do after school?

Did you
have a lot of
homework?
Did you always
do it?

Tell me one of your funniest memories of school.

What were your favorite subjects in school? Your least favorite?

Did you want to pursue a higher education? Did your parents want the same for you?

ABOUT GROWING UP AND
BECOMING AN ADULT

What did you think of high school? _____

_____

_____

_____

_____

_____

_____

_____

_____

_____

_____

Did learning come easily to you, or was it hard? _____

_____

_____

_____

_____

_____

_____

_____

_____

If you had the chance to organize a reunion, who would definitely get an invitation?

What were the most important world events as you were growing up?

ABOUT GROWING UP AND BECOMING AN ADULT

What were you like as a teenager? How did you see the world? _____

_____

_____

_____

_____

_____

_____

_____

_____

_____

_____

_____

_____

What did you look like? What styles were cool back then? _____

_____

_____

_____

_____

_____

_____

Did you try to fit in with a particular group or clique?

What were your dreams back then?

Did you
set any
goals for
yourself?

ABOUT GROWING UP AND
BECOMING AN ADULT

Who did you look up to growing up? Who were your idols?

What were your hobbies? Sports, music, collections?

What was your favorite band or artist?

_____ Did you get an allowance, or did you have a job to earn some extra money?

How much
spending
money did
you have
each week?

_____ What was your first real job?

_____ How old were you when you started working? Do you remember how much you made?

What did
you spend
your first
paycheck on?

ABOUT GROWING UP AND BECOMING AN ADULT

What later jobs did you hold? _____

\
\
\
\
\
\
\
\
\
\
\

Which of your jobs did you like most? Why? _____

\
\
\
\
\
\
\
\
\
\
\
\

How did your views on money change as you got older?

When it comes to education and working, what is your most valuable advice for me?

a page for
pictures . . .

a page for
pictures . . .

... and more stories
and memories

TELL ME SOMETHING
ABOUT ME

What was I like as a kid?

Who did
I resemble
more, you
or Dad?

Did you have a pet name for me?

What did you like most about me as a child?

Which memories from when I was young bring a smile to your face?

TELL ME SOMETHING
ABOUT ME

How do I remind you of your parents?

Did I resemble you more or less as I grew up?

How can
you tell?

What was my favorite food? What food did I hate?

What did I like most about my birthdays?

Do you remember what I thought of my first day of school?

TELL ME SOMETHING ABOUT ME

What family trips or vacations were special to me?

What music did I like when I was little?

What did I want to be when I was all grown up?

What was I like as a teenager? What was the hardest part about that time for you?

And what was
the best part?

a page for
pictures . . .

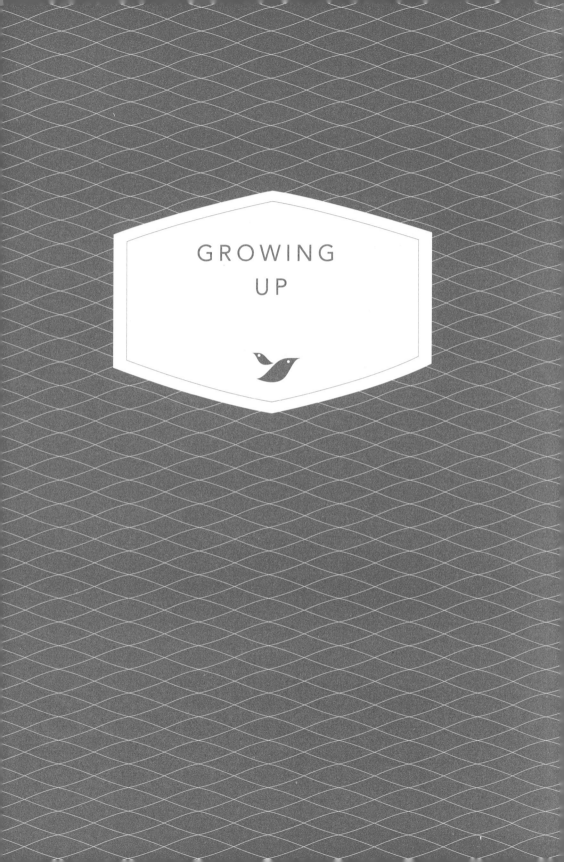

GROWING
UP

ABOUT LOVE

Who was your first crush? When and where did you meet? _____

_____

_____

_____

_____

_____

_____

Who was your first kiss? Did you enjoy the experience? _____

_____

_____

_____

_____

_____

_____

Did you find it easy to talk to your crushes, or were you very shy? _____

_____

_____

_____

_____

_____

_____

Who gave you "the talk"? How old were you?

Who was your first true love?

How did you two meet?

ABOUT LOVE

Have you had many love interests? _____

_____

_____

_____

_____

_____

_____

Did you ever suffer a broken heart? _____

_____

How did you
cope with it? _____

_____

_____

_____

_____

_____

_____

_____

_____

_____

What was the most original or fun way somebody let you know

you were special to them?

How and when did you meet my father?

Was there
an instant
attraction?

ABOUT LOVE

Where did you go on your first date? _____

Were you very
nervous?

When did you really start to fall for him? _____

What did you like most about him?

What did your parents think of him?

Did they
approve of
your choice?

ABOUT LOVE

If you're married, how did he propose? _____

_____

_____

_____

_____

_____

_____

_____

What was your wedding day like? _____

_____

_____

_____

_____

_____

_____

How long have you two been together? _____

_____

_____

_____

What is your best advice for maintaining a healthy relationship?

And what are the biggest pitfalls in a relationship?

a page for
pictures . . .

. . . and more stories
and memories

a page for
pictures . . .

ABOUT BECOMING
A MOTHER

Have you always wanted to be a mom? _____

_____

_____

Was there a
moment you
knew you
were ready
for it?

_____

_____

_____

_____

_____

How did you find out you were pregnant with me? _____

Do you remember how it made you feel? _____

_____

_____

_____

_____

_____

_____

_____

How did Dad deal with the pregnancy?

Did he go to
any classes
with you, for
example?

What was important to you both when it came to raising me?

79

ABOUT BECOMING
A MOTHER

Did you know whether I was going to be a boy or a girl? _____

Was it an easy pregnancy? _____

What were
the moments
you cherished?
Were there any
difficulties?

Did your relationship with your parents change when you were pregnant?

Where did you give birth to me? Was this planned?

What moment will you never forget?

ABOUT BECOMING
A MOTHER

Which people were important to you after you gave birth?

How did your life change after you had me?

How did motherhood change you?

What did you like most about being a mother? And least?

a page for
pictures . . .

. . . and more stories
and memories

a page for
pictures . . .

TELL ME SOMETHING
ABOUT ME

Do you remember who my first love was? What did you think of him/her?

Did I behave differently when I was in love?

Did that change with each new crush?

What is your best advice when it comes to raising children?

Raising me, is there anything you would do differently now,

if you had the chance?

TELL ME SOMETHING
ABOUT ME

Considering everything I have learned from you,

what are you most proud of having taught me?

What has the experience of raising me taught you?

a page for
pictures . . .

. . . and more stories
and memories

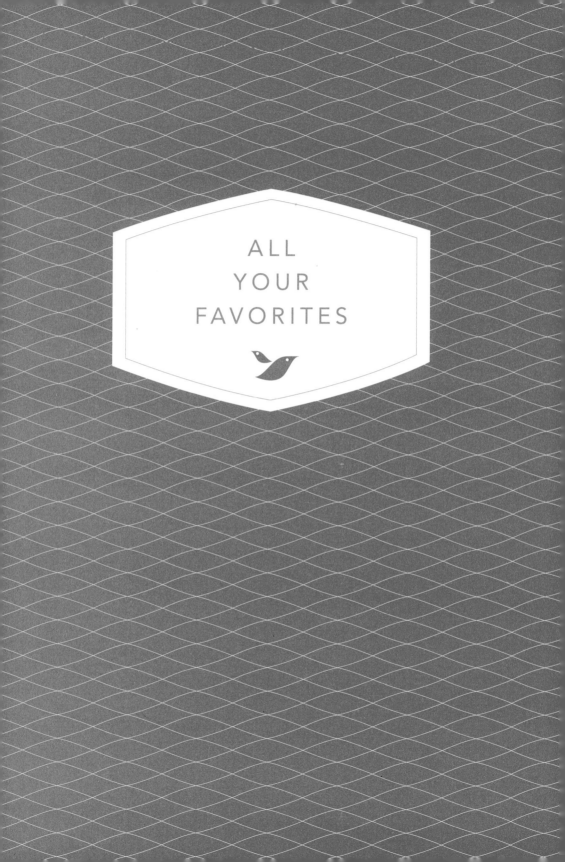

ALL
YOUR
FAVORITES

ABOUT SPARE TIME, HOBBIES, AND TRAVELING

How do you like to spend your weekends?

How did you like to spend your weekends when you were younger?

How old were
you when
you started
going out?

What were your favorite hangouts?

Who did
you go
out with?

What are some of your favorite memories from back then?

ABOUT SPARE TIME,
HOBBIES, AND TRAVELING

How do you spend your free time?

Do you enjoy reading?

What
are your
favorite
books?

What was the first movie you saw in a theater?

What are your favorite movies?

What makes you so excited you'd drop everything to talk about it?

ABOUT SPARE TIME, HOBBIES, AND TRAVELING

What are your favorite TV shows?

And which ones make you reach for the remote?

If you could eat at any restaurant, which one would you choose?

What is your favorite food?

What are your favorite travel destinations?

ABOUT SPARE TIME, HOBBIES, AND TRAVELING

When you're on vacation, what do you miss from home?

What was one of your best trips? Why?

And which vacation was just plain awful? What happened?

Which places do you feel everyone should visit at least once in their lifetime?

ABOUT SPARE TIME,
HOBBIES, AND TRAVELING

What music never fails to cheer you up?

What is the best or most beautiful thing about the country where you live?

What would you do if you won a million dollars?

a page for
pictures . . .

a page for
pictures . . .

... and more stories
and memories

TELL ME SOMETHING ABOUT ME

What was our first vacation together like? Where did we go?

What things would you still like to see or do with me?

Why these
things in
particular?

Did you read to me when I was young?

Which books were my favorites?

Is there anything you think I should absolutely read,

listen to, or do when I get the chance?

a page for
pictures . . .

... and more stories
and memories

a page for
pictures . . .

. . . and more stories
and memories

WHO YOU ARE NOW

ABOUT MEMORIES

Is there a particular song, scent, or something else that never _____

fails to remind you of something wonderful? _____

_____

_____

_____

_____

_____

_____

_____

_____

_____

_____

Which of your dreams came true? _____

_____

Which of
your dreams
would you still
like to
come true?

_____

_____

_____

_____

_____

Which of your accomplishments in life makes you feel proud?

What would you still like to accomplish?

What life lesson would you like to pass on to me?

ABOUT MEMORIES

Is there a joke or funny memory that still makes you laugh to this day?

What are the best decisions you've made in your life?

What obstacles did have you overcome in your life?

How did
you do this?

ABOUT MEMORIES

What are your regrets, big or small? _____

_____

_____

_____

_____

_____

_____

_____

_____

_____

What is the best resolution you ever made? _____

_____

_____

_____

_____

_____

_____

_____

If you had the chance, which moments in your life

would you like to live all over again?

What do you think are the most remarkable events in history

that happened during your life?

ABOUT MEMORIES

Which historical figures do you admire?

Which people in your life do you owe a lot to?

Who did you
learn the
most from?

What is the biggest difference between who you used to be and

who you are now?

Were there any important people in your life you had to say good-bye to?

How did
you deal
with that
loss?

a page for
pictures . . .

... and more stories
and memories

127

a page for
pictures . . .

ABOUT THOUGHTS,
WISHES, AND DREAMS

What do you think are the most important things in life?

How important is your home to you?

What's your
favorite spot
at home?

Who serves as an inspiration to you?

Why this
person?

Which famous people do you admire?

ABOUT THOUGHTS, WISHES, AND DREAMS

Which days of the year are important to you?

How do you
like to spend
these days?

And which traditions do you love?

What does happiness mean to you?

Did you
always look
at it that
way?

What are your best qualities?

ABOUT THOUGHTS, WISHES, AND DREAMS

What would you change about yourself if you could?

What things would you still like to learn?

What do you think are some of the benefits of growing older?

What makes you howl with laughter?

ABOUT THOUGHTS,
WISHES, AND DREAMS

What things really move you? _____

_____

_____

_____

_____

_____

_____

_____

_____

What is your favorite day of the week? And your favorite month of the year? _____

_____

_____

_____

_____

_____

_____

_____

If you could rule the world for one day, what would be your first decision?

In what ways has the world changed as you have grown older?

ABOUT THOUGHTS,
WISHES, AND DREAMS

What does friendship mean to you?

Who are your
best friends?
Why is that?

What is the greatest gift someone could give you?

Who helps you pull through when life gets tough?

What is one of the biggest compliments you have ever received?

ABOUT THOUGHTS, WISHES, AND DREAMS

What places or countries would you still like to visit?

Looking back, what were the greatest moments in your life?

Which great moments are still to come?

Is there anything you would still like to tell me?

a page for
pictures . . .

. . . and more stories
and memories

a page for
pictures . . .

... and more stories
and memories

TELL ME SOMETHING
ABOUT ME

Which of my choices makes you proud?

What have you learned from me?

Which of our moments together would you pick
if you could go back and relive them?

TELL ME SOMETHING ABOUT ME

What is the most wonderful thing about our relationship? _____

What would make it even better? _____

Are there any questions you would like to ask me? _____

What dreams do you have for me?

a page for
pictures . . .

. . . and more stories
and memories

PENGUIN BOOKS

An imprint of Penguin Random House LLC
375 Hudson Street
New York, New York 10014
penguinrandomhouse.com

Published in Dutch as *Mam, vertel eens* by
Spectrum, an imprint of Uitgeverij Unieboek,
Houten, Netherlands

A product by Elma van Vliet
Original cover and design by Julia Brants, Den Haag.
Cover modified by Nayon Chu.

ISBN 9780143133742

Printed in the United States of America
10 9 8 7 6 5 4 3 2 1

Set in Chaparral Pro
Designed by Julia Brants